MEDITATIONS FOR

SINGLE
MOMS

Herald Press
Meditation Books

By Helen Good Brenneman
Meditations for the Expectant Mother
Meditations for the New Mother

By John M. Drescher
Meditations for the Newly Married

By Vernell Klassen Miller
Meditations for Adoptive Parents

By Gerald and Sara Wenger Shenk
Meditations for New Parents

By Larry Wilson
Daily Fellowship with God

By Various Authors
Visitation Pamphlet Series

MEDITATIONS FOR

SINGLE MOMS

SUSANNE COALSON DONOGHUE

HERALD PRESS
Scottdale, Pennsylvania
Waterloo, Ontario

Library of Congress Cataloging-in-Publication Data
Donoghue, Susanne Coalson, 1945-
     Meditations for single moms / Susanne Coalson Donoghue.
       p. cm.
     Includes bibliographical references.
     ISBN 0-8361-9061-0 (alk. paper)
     1. Single mothers—Prayer-books and devotions—English.
I. Title.
BV4596.S48D66 1997
242'.6431—dc21   96-51876

The paper used in this publication is recycled and meets the minimum require-
ments of American National Standard for Information Sciences—Permanence of
Paper for Printed Library Materials, ANSI Z39.48-1984.

All Bible quotations are used by permission, all rights reserved, and are from the
The Holy Bible, New International Version, copyright © 1973, 1978, 1984
International Bible Society, Zondervan Bible Publishers.

MEDITATIONS FOR SINGLE MOMS
Copyright © 1997 by Herald Press, Scottdale, Pa. 15683
     Published simultaneously in Canada by Herald Press,
     Waterloo, Ont. N2L 6H7. All rights reserved
Library of Congress Catalog Number: 96-51876
International Standard Book Number: 0-8361-9061-0
Printed in the United States of America
Cover design by Paula M. Johnson

05 04 03 02 01 00 99 98 97 10 9 8 7 6 5 4 3 2 1

For Vincent, without whose love and belief
this book could not have been written.

For Elspeth and Shoshanna,
who taught me most of what I know.

And for Anne and the other single moms
who have shared this journey of faith.

Contents

Author's Preface

*Fear not, you shall not be put to shame; you need not blush, for you
shall not be disgraced. The shame of your youth you shall forget,
the reproach of your widowhood no longer remember. For he who has
become your husband is your Maker; his name is the Lord of hosts;
your redeemer is the Holy One of Israel,
called God of all the earth.*
Isaiah 54:4-5

Many paths lead to single parenthood, and more and more people
are on those paths. The Census Bureau reports that in 1990 there were 9.7
million single parents in the United States. Eighty-four percent, or
8,350,000, were single mothers (*USA Today*, June 14, 1991). This does
not account for the noncustodial single parents who are involved to vary-
ing degrees in raising their children.

I personally came to single parenthood by a path which burdened
me with a great deal of shame. My daughter's father was married to someone else. Although my experience is not unique, we single parents are a
diverse group. Death, abandonment, or hospitalization of one parent
produce millions of families whose children have no experience of fathering, or in a smaller number of cases, of mothering. Divorce or parents
not living together produces millions more in which children experience
fathering or mothering separately, in different environments, and for
shorter periods of time. Depending on the children's ages at the time of
their parents' divorce or separation, death or illness, they may also experience significant and abrupt change in their experience of mothering or
fathering. They may understand the reasons for the change—or they may
never understand.

What are we as Christians to make of all this? We find ourselves in
this category, "single parent," with all its attendant bad press. Many of us
did not choose to be there. Perhaps for some of us parenting seemed the
lesser of two evils, but what is a choice between two evils if not a dilem-
ma? How are we to teach our children? Will they turn out all right?

When I learned I was pregnant, I panicked. I felt unequipped to be a parent, let alone a single parent. How would I provide all that my daughter needed from a mother and a father? How would we survive? In the midst of my despair, God spoke to me, planting thoughts in my mind as God often does: "It will be all right."

The panic disappeared. I began to face my life. I heard the words from Isaiah 54 (above) as if spoken to me personally. God became partner, father, protector, provider. He brought us to a small church 2,000 miles from home; there we were welcomed and taught. My relationship with Jesus grew and strengthened, so I found much healing from the self-hatred, loneliness, and rejection that had propelled me into disastrous relationships.

Through this painful and traumatic experience, I have learned that God is real and truly present; that I can always talk to God and God to me; that God is totally dependable in a way no man or woman can ever be. I have been enabled to put my trust in Jesus and have never been disappointed.

Over two decades ago, God promised, "It will be all right." Because of God's gracious love and forgiveness, it has been so.

I have talked to dozens of others who came to being single parents by different paths. No one says the road is easy. But all report that their faith in God is their most important health and survival resource, more important than job, financial security, even the support of family or friends.

In these pages, I hope to share some of that faith with you. Not everyone has come to this place by the same road, but we all have the same heavenly Parent in whom we can trust, and grow, and thrive. God's peace to you.

—*Susanne Coalson Donoghue*
Evanston, Illinois

THE GIFT OF PAIN

If there were butterflies in February
Or hummingbirds in March,
Flocks of emerald and scarlet, gold and turquoise
Would so assault our sleeping senses,
Buried in snow and benumbed by ice-gray skies,
We would not survive the shock.

"It cannot be all candy clouds,"
The mother tells her child,
"Or you would be sick of sweetness,"
But the child disdains her wisdom,
Pouting under blankets and TV and books,
Refusing to come out.

And I would, too, except I remember
Skies afloat with swarms of golden butterflies
Swerving and lofting above the iris' royal cloaks;
And call to mind the cloud-borne anointing, reviving,
Of the green land fainting under scourge of solar armies;
And the tears of the surrendering soldier,
Delivered from the uncertainties of war;
And my own tears of unbelieving joy
On my wedding day.

In the providence of God,
Hope is Pain's daughter;
And so I go out to meet the inimical day,
Chill, bluster, ice and all;
And I decree like a queen of old,
"Show me your gift."

MEDITATIONS FOR

SINGLE MOMS

Saying Yes

You will be with child and give birth to a son,
and you are to give him the name Jesus.
He will be great and will be called the
Son of the Most High.
Luke 1:31-32

It occurred to me once that in the eyes of those around her, Mary's virginity was probably dubious. Never mind them, we say. The angel never spoke to them. We know the truth.

However, Mary probably had to deal with their doubts anyway. I thought of this because at the time I became pregnant, the Lord had highlighted Luke 1:31-32 for me in a special way, and I was resisting the idea that these words might apply to my child, too. Unlike Mary, I had sinned.

I was brought to understand that these verses point to the importance of every birth. God has a name for every child even before he or she is born—and not only a name but a special assignment.

Each child born is intended by God as a gift to the world. Each child is handpicked and custom-designed to bless the receiving world. It is not the child's fault, but the world's, if the gift is rejected, and it is the world's loss as well. If received, every child is necessary to the well-being of its parents and the planet. It seems to me that a good deal of what is wrong with the world comes from children (and adults) believing they are not really needed. This is a *lie*.

I have never liked the term *illegitimate child*—as if the child were at fault for being born. God was saying to me through this verse, "I legitimate this child; I have chosen her to be born and to be the one to bless you and, in a special way, the earth."

My friend, Anne, an African-American single parent, says that she was raised in small-town Mississippi to believe it was her job to "prepare myself to advance the race."

What if every child knew without question that he or she was born to be great, to be the child of the Most High, and to "get ready to advance" the human race?

SAYING YES

Child within,
Memory of the child that was,
You still hurt;
You still grieve alone
That the beauty of you was never seen,
That the miracle of you was never shared.

Child within,
You are the life-seed,
The God-seed,
Sent into the world
Which knew you not
Nor wanted to,
Locking you up in the cold and dark
To die.

Little one,
I hold you.
Come into the warm light.
Burrow down into my embrace.
Sprout, little one, grow.
I protect you.
I will water you with my tears.
I want to see you thrive and bud,
Bloom and cast your seeds
Into the mothering earth.
I do love you so.

To a Young Mother

She named him Samuel, saying,
"Because I asked the Lord for him. . . .
So now I give him to the Lord.
For his whole life he will be
given over to the Lord."
1 Samuel 1:20, 28

Samuel means, roughly "The Lord heard me." The name the angel Gabriel gave to Mary's Son means "God saves." Our names tell us about ourselves and our lives. Like our lives, they are gifts from our parents and from God as well. Once I knew that a child had entered into life within me, I began to search for a name to welcome this new person.

The responsibility of welcoming this little one all by myself was overwhelming. How would he or she feel about my not providing for a father? How would I, alone, provide enough for this child—enough money, enough love, enough discipline, enough security? Into my terrified mind dropped these words of quiet authority, "It will be all right." I would not be alone. God gives and sustains life. I chose my daughter's name to remind us both of this. It means "God has promised."

Nearly two decades later, I still do not know how my daughter will judge my decisions regarding her life, but I do know God has been faithful to that long-ago promise, "It will be all right." To keep it, God used resources inconceivable to me at the time. God hears the prayers we are not as bold as Hannah to voice, even the requests we feel are too presumptuous to make. Hears—and answers.

TO A YOUNG MOTHER

Do not be afraid, young one,
That you are too young,
That you are not ready,
That you are alone.

For I am God,
Your mother and your father,
Life-giver and the source of your life.
And I am with you.

With me you are strong.
With me you are loved.
And you are chosen
To give birth and life.

I will be with you.
You shall lack nothing.
You will enter into the heart of the mystery of life,
And I promise you, you shall be satisfied.

Be at peace,
I am with you now
In the sunlight, in the air, in the song of birds,
In the love of friends.

And I will be with you,
I will be with you, believe me,
I will be with you,
Until the end of time.

The World Has Beaten Me

*"Sing, O barren woman, you who never bore a child . . .
because more are the children of the desolate woman
than of her who has a husband," says the Lord.*
Isaiah 54:1

Bearing my load of shame and fear, I entered the enormous sanctuary late and crept into the nearest pew. Several thousand people gathering for worship make a certain anonymity possible. To me it was welcome. I knew the Lord had at last answered my prayers and delivered me from this sinful relationship, but I did not know how he felt about me and my weakness. Now I was pregnant as well. The church had condemned me. How did God feel?

The words above, read from the pulpit, snapped me to attention. I knew they were metaphoric, speaking of Israel. But they seemed also to be addressed to me personally. I had hidden in this sea of 3,000 people, hoping just to hear God's word from a distance, daring to approach no closer. Instead, the Holy Spirit was speaking directly "to my condition," as the Friends say.

I had never been inside this church before. Their custom was to read straight through the Bible from beginning to end, commenting on the text as they went. There is not a passage in the entire canon which could have spoken to me more personally.

"For a brief moment I abandoned you, but with deep compassion I will bring you back" (v. 7). Had I worried about how God felt about me? "Though the mountains be shaken and the hills be removed, yet my unfailing love for you will not be shaken nor my covenant of peace be removed,' says the Lord, who has compassion on you" (v. 10).

Had I really heard God say it would be all right? "All your sons will be taught by the Lord, and great will be your children's peace" (v. 13).

Though these words were written thousands of years before, they were addressed to people who, like me, had been unfaithful, who had sinned and done what they knew was wrong.

I no longer felt like the one sinner in a crowd of people with clean hands. Even if I were, God loved me. I no longer feared my child would be punished for my sin. God was holding out to me not punishment but redemption, an invitation to come back, and a promise of unfailing love.

THE WORLD HAS BEATEN ME

The world has beaten me,
Stripped me naked
And driven me out,
And the wolves prowl,
Waiting their turn.

Bare and shivering,
No door but yours
Would open to me—
And I was afraid to come,
Ashamed of myself.

When I came at last
In very desperation,
Your door stood open.
Unnerved, I cringed outside,
Gaping speechless at the light.
You drew me in,
Covered my flinching body,
Held me close without speaking.
No words could add
To the welcome in your eyes.
Oh, why did I wait so long?

And why,
When I find myself once more
Wandering unclothed in the snow,
Do I forget where you live,
For very shame of coming
This way to you again
And of what people will think?

Your eyes are always the same,
Your arms as welcoming as before.

I am ashamed.
And you draw me in.
"Stay," your eyes say.
I could gaze into them forever,
It seems, transfixed by your greeting.
"I will never let you go,"
Your arms say,
And the rejected one in me,
Astonished,
Unfolds her trampled petals.
"You want me?"

"The world beat me, too,"
You say, "stripped me naked
And drove me out.
Your worth to me
Is the same as mine to you.
More, I expect."
Your smile at that is like the dawning.

Lord, may I see your face ever before me,
And when I glance away,
May I always look back.
May I never wander;
But when I do,
May I come home.
And may my door
Always be wide
To your poverty and want
When you appear, shivering
In your guise as stranger;
And when it is shut,
May I hear your tears and open.

Jerusalem, Jerusalem

Jerusalem, Jerusalem, you who kill the prophets and stone those sent to you, how often have I longed to gather your children together, as a hen gathers her chicks under her wings, but you were not willing.
Matthew 23:37

I watch her from a distance, not to alarm her.
She does not know I am here.
I send her gifts to please her;
She ignores them.
I can see them piled up around her door
Even from here.
She goes in and out with her fond friends
And never sees my gifts, never sees me.
I could yet be content in my pain
If she were happy.
At night I pass by the lighted windows,
Feeling that strange tug of anguish as I look upon her separateness.
She who is my world has become a foreign land.
When the lights go out, and the stars are sharp and cold,
If I pass very near, I can hear her crying.
If only she would let me in,
So gladly would I comfort her!
I think sometimes my heart will break;
But then, it is already broken.

So morning comes—my gift, unreceived.
She dresses in bright colors, puts on her brave lipstick
And strides purposefully into her day,
Ignoring the drifts of flowers under the brilliant sky.
She used to love them, but now they do not exist for her.

I could cancel them all out,
Leaving her and me alone in the universe, face-to-face;
But still she would not love me.
Instead I do the only two things I know how—
And oh! how practiced I have become, too—
Love her and wait.

One day—it may be—
And none shall forbid me hope—
She will turn—perhaps today!—
And see me waiting here,
Loving her,
As ardently as the sun loves the earth
And calls it into being.

And perhaps—oh, I know how wild it seems,
But it could be—
She will smile and come to me.
And then I will see the hard loneliness in her eyes
Take flight under the burning gaze of my passion,
And she will find herself met
For the first time
By a love big enough to hold her.
And perhaps she will not pass by in scorn then
As she did so many years ago
When I stretched out my arms to her in love
On the fiery Roman bed she made for me of wood and iron and gall
Outside the walls of Jerusalem.
I can endure her surprise at my constancy,
I can endure my own pain,
If only she will recognize my love and take it in.

Is that something new I see in her eyes?
Is there a restlessness? Is she weary of evading me?
Might I kindle hope in her now?
Could this be the day? I must see!

For your Maker is your husband—the Lord Almighty is his name—the Holy One of Israel is your Redeemer; he is called the God of all the earth.
Isaiah 54:5

Alone. The most frightening word in the English language. To most women—and men—to be utterly and completely alone is like a sentence of death. To be a parent alone . . . unthinkable.

For two years, my daughter and I lived in a two-room cabin on my aunt's and uncle's property, four miles from the nearest very small (pop. 978) town. My family was appalled. I am grateful to them for doing most of their worrying behind my back. The truth was that I needed the solitude. Like a wounded thing, I had crept deep into the forest with my baby to hide until I could heal.

I had wanted to be married, longed for a partner to share every bit of life. I had even been married and then deserted, not once but twice. The pain of being abandoned a third time was so intense I walked through the days sighing, "Oh Lord, how long?" Then, "Oh Lord, you alone know." Know what? Know the pain I feel. Know the loneliness. Know how I will ever survive this. Know what's wrong with me. Know the future—will it always be like this? I had no other words to speak.

Day after day, "Oh Lord, you know." From outward appearances, we were alone, profoundly so. The silver foxes and the quail they hunted went about their business unaware of our presence. The deer in their ghostly way passed through our clearing never knowing I watched them. I wrote poems and slipped them into the file folder where they rested unseen for years.

I joined a church and people visited me, but sensitively. They were kind, especially the minister and his wife. My aunt and uncle and their children were generous with their time and resources. My mother died suddenly. All were gracious and supportive. I joined a small women's prayer group in which we could share and cry and pray. All those relationships were healing.

The most important healing was hidden. The Lord was approaching me with offers of love and fidelity. "I will be your husband," he said. I have to confess, I was afraid I was losing my mind. I had read about crazy women who talked of mystical experiences and a divine Lover. I went to a local minister who encouraged people to "listen to the Lord" and told him what the Lord seemed to be saying to me. He responded, "If the Lord wants to write love poems to you all day long, who am I to argue with him?"

I was startled and amused. Who was *I* to question him? Sixteen years later, it makes sense. I had been rejected—God wanted me. My image of marriage was similar to the relationship God wants to have with his people—total commitment, complete sharing, confidence and trust. God answered my longing, not literally, but in substance. I was not alone, never had been, never would be.

I could feel sad, and sigh, "Oh Lord, you know." In the confidence that the Lord heard me and did indeed understand and even respond to me was the healing of my deep wounds.

Years later, I still think of the Lord as my husband—and spouse of us all. I think of God as faithful, loving, committed, protecting, preserving, nurturing, comforting, and strong. Without God, it would be folly to form any relationship, given my weakness, ignorance, and limited love. God has offered us this covenant of grace. It would be unspeakable folly to refuse.

Bedtime Prayers

He gives strength to the weary and increases the power of the weak.
Even youths grow tired and weary, and young men stumble and fall;
but those who hope in the Lord will renew their strength.
They will soar on wings like eagles; they will run and not
grow weary, they will walk and not be faint.
Isaiah 40:29-31

Let's have a look at Brother Donkey, shall we? Freely I borrow St. Francis' image for the body. He is so rich now, he won't mind. I cannot recall the name of the writer who suggested that one's physical body is the gift of a merciful God, a companion to help carry the incredible burden of the soul.

Parenting is physically exhausting! Decades ago, a national magazine hired professional football players in top physical condition to imitate all the activities of young children. All the pros were done in before the end of the day; the kids were still going strong. Is it any wonder parents, especially single parents, get so tired?

When my daughter was small, I used to live for nap time. I slept every time she did. How I mourned when the afternoon nap became obsolete! In fact, she now accuses me of putting her to bed when I, and not she, needed to sleep. Never forget that nursing a baby is severely depleting your physical resources as well!

Parents learn that if we neglect Brother Donkey, there is soon nothing left with which to care for others. We learn that the tasks of feeding and resting and exercising and bathing Brother Donkey, homely as they are, are also holy tasks through which we learn gratefully to receive God's gift of the body. Performing these tasks is a gift as well to our children (who imitate us) and to those around us, who otherwise are compelled to bear Brother Donkey's soul burdens because he is too weak from neglect to do it himself.

Today if feeling crabby or sulky, I check first with Brother Donkey. Is he hungry, thirsty, sleepy, or uncomfortable? Every parent quickly learns the baby has different sounding cries, usually by changing the diaper instead of feeding the ravenous child. We learn as well that nothing will stop the crying until the need is met! The same is true of Brother Donkey.

Sometimes Sister Soul tries to make Brother Donkey carry too much. Then Brother Donkey brays and carries on to wake the dead. We feel embarrassed, think he should be stronger, that we've got a lazy donkey.

Those are the times Sister Soul needs to turn to God in prayer and realize it is not all up to her. As we hope in God and realize our creature-hood, our dependence on heaven for everything, our strength is renewed —a strength which can only be realized in weakness (as Paul noted in 2 Cor. 12:9).

BEDTIME PRAYERS

I am a tangled necklace,
Hopelessly knotted and snarled.
Clasp unfurled,
I lie in a heap so twisted
Sleep brings no rest.

Patiently my Jesus works,
Night after night,
Sorts my thoughts, smoothes my feelings,
Cleanses me, ravels knots
Till all is order and shining.
So patient!—although
It will never be different.
There will always be knots.

He never tires, sorting them out,
Because he loves order and shining.
Who is so patient as my Lord?
I coil my mind about him
And rest. All is well.

Trying to Be Still

If any of you lacks wisdom, he should ask God, who gives generously to all without finding fault, and it will be given to him.
James 1:5

I remember one Saturday when my daughter was two, I was so exhausted from the day's labor that by suppertime all I could do was stand and stare into the lighted interior of the refrigerator. I had lugged the fifteen-gallon diaper pail full of water and dirty diapers and also the holding tank for the chemical toilet to my aunt's (fully-plumbed) home; done the laundry there; come home to pick up toys, to vacuum, and to load up the baby to go grocery shopping. My brain was as good as dead.

I stood looking in the refrigerator for a long time, unable to form the wispiest notion of a supper.

Some disdain prayers at such a time. Not I!

"Help me, Lord," I cried. "What shall I fix for dinner?"

Quick as lightning came the reply, "What about a peanut-butter-and-jelly sandwich?"

For *dinner?* You must be joking!

I was astonished and delighted. What an amazing thought. Lunch anytime! Thinking of dinner in terms of meat, potatoes, and vegetables, and failing to come up with that, I was stuck. But God broke through the mental barriers—the axioms of "proper" nutrition and my mother's patterns—and pointed to the basics.

The new energy pouring into me was wonderful. It came from knowing God was with me, that God understood and accepted my incapacity, that God cared about my weariness and was ready with an inexhaustible supply of energy whenever I began to flag. It came from knowing that many of God's answers, like this one, would be a complete surprise, creatively bypassing my preconceived and limiting ideas and categories. Often they seem outrageously simple.

I call these PBJ prayers now—the ones when I am stuck and can't find a way out. God answers these delightedly and, in the words of the King James Version, "upbraideth not." That means God doesn't yank your hair, as some of my grade school teachers did to control their students. God is delighted to share wisdom with us and pleased that we asked. Just don't be surprised if the wisdom comes in an unorthodox package! God always uses what happens to be on hand.

TRYING TO BE STILL

I am still. Because I do not know what to do.
Waiting. Because I do not know where to go.
My breath comes slow,
Wasting nothing.
Mimicking death, I listen.
Which way does the holy wind blow?
Might I become so light and so empty
It will carry me to my unguessed end?

Oh, the stillness is mockery:
Life flows busily on inside me,
Each milliamp of exchange
Belying my kenosis.
"It is not possible!" I cry,
Even as the holy wind touches my face
And begins to lift me.

Single Parent

*Are not two sparrows sold for a penny? Yet not one of them will fall
to the ground apart from the will of your Father. And even the very
hairs of your head are all numbered. So don't be afraid;
you are worth more than many sparrows.*
Matthew 10:29-31

Three of my brothers are noncustodial single parents through divorce. Alex has custody of his son only on weekends and a few weeks in the summer. He said to me a few years ago that he did not know what he would do if he couldn't pray. He worries about his son and not being there for him all week.

When he brings these worries to God, his heavenly Father reassures him, "I'm looking out for him, don't forget. I know what it's like to worry about a son."

When his son is with Alex, they make the most of their time. They go on family fishing trips in the summer (men-only affairs involving my dad and all my brothers who can make it). Alex can almost always be reached at home on weekends, where I discover them working on homework from school, decorating the house for Christmas, even cooking together. They talk about everything, Alex tells me. He's especially interested in what to say on the topic of girls. And his son is turning out to be a very fine boy.

Alex is sure it's because God is looking out for them, as promised.

I think so, too.

SINGLE PARENT

Dear Lord,
I am worried about my daughter.

You, I know, are worried about Haiti and some others as well.

Can we just sit here and be worried together?
Do you think we did the right thing
Bringing them into the world?

The risks are so great—
Surely you know that better than anyone.
Can you give me any hope?

You promised me it would be all right.
What does "all right" mean?

And of course,
There's the woman who suffered so much in her life,
Especially from the things that didn't happen.

The worst thing would be if she never grew up
Because I made her so afraid to try. Don't let me do that.

Is there any hope I can give her?
There are my wonderful friends—
And if I could be happy about my place in the world,
And undaunted by the pain I have suffered,
There would be that.

Help me, Lord. I'm not as good a parent as you.
My faith department is understaffed, too.

You told me it would be all right. I trust you, too,
Even though I know for every resurrection,
There must first be a crucifixion.
What does "all right" look like?
Still learning, not failing.
Confidence unharmed.
Walking toward love and light,
Away from darkness and fear.

She is very brave, I know that.
I must believe in her, too.
Believe in the promise
That a woman is a good thing,
Giving birth a good thing,
That a child is a good thing. Yes, I do.
Keep it in front of me.

Cloud of Witnesses

*I have swept away your offenses like a cloud, your sins like the
morning mist. Return to me, for I have redeemed you.*
Isaiah 44:22

Ask any parent what role guilt plays in the relationship with his or her children. Likely you will get an earful. The same applies double for single parents.

My daughter asked me once, "Mom, didn't you ever think of how it would be for me not to have a dad?" I had to reply that all such thoughts, and there were many, had come after her conception. Ouch!

God had forgiven me. But my daughter had to forgive me, too. Harder still, I had to forgive myself. It is unhealthy for them and for us to relate to our children out of guilt. Yet we are *all* guilty. Have you ever heard of the Society for Children of Perfect Parents? Neither have I. Yet this image of "The Way It's Spozed to Be" tyrannizes so many of us.

We find it much easier to forgive our children. "They'll learn," we say. We believe the heartfelt assurances they give us: "We're sorry. We didn't mean it. We won't do it again." When they do it again, we may become concerned for their *ability* to learn to do better, but rarely do we view the child as an incorrigible sinner, a hopeless case.

My downstairs neighbor, father of five grown children, said to me recently, "It helped me a great deal to realize that it isn't part of the deal for us to get through the process of raising kids without sin."

Both their sins and ours are, in his phrase, "part of the deal."

How do we live with this truth? I believe God views us similarly to how we view our children when they make mistakes. The whole business of life is not about succeeding or failing, not about avoiding error and fault. Those are a given. From God's point of view, we are like children. Mistakes and faults are part of life: the goal of life is learning to know and love God and each other. We are all of us, parent and child, learners.

If we can see that, keep it in mind, then we can accept God's release from blame or punishment for our faults. We can approach our true Parent as tiny children, asking and expecting to be taught, helped, and healed. As an added bonus, our chidren learn to approach God in the same way.

CLOUD OF WITNESSES

My friend and I packed china today.
Her people from the Old South and mine from the Dust Bowl,
We found ourselves trailing dreams of our foremothers
Like bits of newspaper and twine.

Some of her sugar bowls belonged to her grandmother,
Perhaps the first generation out of slavery
To own such things instead of washing another's.
My own mother's mother, fleeing an alcoholic father's rage,
Never had such riches, though she must have dreamed of them.

We spent the morning in their presence, amiably,
Not needing talk. Like Roman matrons polishing the family shrine,
We wrapped and nudged and poked each small package into its nest,
While around us whispered the dreams of women long gone.

Surely plastic plates are more practical,
And who needs a service for twelve these days?
But such considerations were strangely immaterial
In the face of the realized hopes of the poor.
Plate after teacup reminded us that though times change and we with them,
We are securely anchored in the tides of generations,
Ebb and flow, a new one and a newer.
Never mind, we are all connected—by hope, by courage,
And the power of the seed to grow and the heart to heal.

And mothers of ours, for all you did for us, for good or for ill,
We salute you; touch with compassion, respect, and a kind of sorrow
The shapes of beauty or ugliness your earthly dreams took.
For we are that, too, and we ourselves know we never meant
To chip or crack or harm anything you set store by, though we did.
And sometimes we were forced to abandon what you gave us,
But never you, mothers, as long as we draw breath;
Never abandon you with your dreams and your loneliness,
Your secret pride, your stubborn, rooted growing.
Our own dreams have been chipped, cracked, and broken,
And come to denouements we never would have chosen.
But linked to you by roots too deep to wither, we, too, live
And dream and die, come what will.

NINTH DAY

In the Village of God

A father to the fatherless, a defender of widows, is God
in his holy dwelling. God sets the lonely in families,
he leads forth the prisoners with singing.
Psalm 68:5-6

Early in my experience of single parenting, I met a young man whose wife had left him. He was searching for a housekeeper willing to cope with five children, primitive living conditions, low pay, and a herd of milk goats! He very much wanted me to fill this role. Although I needed a job badly, friends advised me to refuse, noting that he was too desperate for me to be able to care for my family's needs and his.

That same year, I met a young woman walking along the freeway, carrying her infant son. She related that she had a chance to become a topless dancer in a distant city. She wanted to take it because it meant a job and maybe someday a husband to help raise her son.

Recently a close friend of mine with two children was abandoned by her husband. She told me that her worst nightmare had come true, since she was now a single parent. Within a few months, she had begun a relationship that looked chancy to those who loved her.

Carrying the responsibilities of two parents is a heavy load for one. When my daughter turned two, I realized how much more she needed than I could provide. I heard about a Christian community in the Midwest; after a month's investigation and much prayer, I moved us there.

This might look like the desperate decisions made by the people I have just described, and you would be right. My family thought I had jumped the track, joining a community in which all income was shared, no one owned his or her own house or car, and all personal decisions were made in consultation with the community. They thought a cult had gotten me.

It has turned out to be a tremendous blessing. Religion that is pure, according to James 1:27 is to "look after orphans and widows in their distress." Folks at Reba Place were practicing a pure religion, in spite of lots of mistakes. My daughter and I have been the grateful beneficiaries, and we have learned from the mistakes as well.

An African proverb says, "It takes two people to make a child, but it takes a whole village to raise it." One of the major difficulties single (and other!) parents in Western culture face is the absence of the village. Through the community, God has been a father to my daughter and a protector for me. The single fathers also, though fewer in number, have experienced God's care through the community.

It is like having dozens of aunts, uncles, and cousins (and even grandparents) caring for us; inviting us for dinner; giving counsel; checking on us during holidays, which can be the worst times; babysitting to give us space for the healing of our grief; and receiving and valuing our contributions to the life of the community. One couple even sent me Valentine's Day cards. The single parents themselves have banded together at times for mutual care and counsel, the older helping the younger.

This was a far better route for me and my daughter than desperately seeking a partner to replace her absent father.

IN THE VILLAGE OF GOD

In the village of God, people cry,
But on another's shoulder.
No child ever cries alone.
People laugh, but not at each other.
They laugh a lot in the village of God,
Because it is always such a surprise
To discover the goodness of God
Hidden away in human hearts.
They cry a lot, too, because so many
Need so much that it hurts,
Need the Father's blessing and the Mother's love,
Need warmth and food and shoes and medicine.
Because they cry together, God hears.
You wouldn't believe all the shoes that appear from nowhere.

Windfall Inheritance

God sets the lonely in families, he leads forth the prisoners with singing,
but the rebellious live in a sun-scorched land.
Psalm 68:6

"Mom," my eight-year-old daughter said to me one Christmas morning, "we aren't a real family."

"Why do you say that?" I asked.

"Because there's just you and me," she replied.

Ouch!

What is a real family? A mom, a dad, children, and a dog? Which part of that formula is essential? I feel strongly that we are a real family, so I told her so. God gave us to each other to exchange love, responsibility, fellowship. She was dubious, although we had family traditions—carols and candlelight on Christmas Eve, stockings and presents on Christmas morning and a phone call to my parents, vacations to see my family each year, birthday celebrations, inviting people who don't have family nearby for Thanksgiving and Easter, homemade cards for special and ordinary occasions, and Saturday chores. We even invented a ritual of our own, which we called "going on a quest"; we get in the car and go until we arrive somewhere we have never been and stop to explore. We learned how to go camping, sometimes inviting friends along.

Several years later, when she was struggling with how deficient our family seemed compared to others, I prayed for God to show me what more I should be doing for her. The astonishing reply: "She doesn't need more from you but from others. She needs time with other families."

So I arranged this, wondering what would happen. Only a few days later, a friend invited her on a camping weekend as a mother's helper. It so happens that my daughter looked on this woman as an ideal mother, with a real family—a husband, three children, a dog, and a cat. She had babysat for them before and jumped at the chance to be with them for the weekend. When she came back, she had learned something I'd tried to teach her years before. "Mom," she said, "Angela lost it and yelled at her kids this weekend. I thought only you did that."

What the Lord knew and I did not was that my daughter needed to know that all real families, even ideal ones, have problems, deficiencies and struggles, just like us. She could only learn that by spending time with other folks in other situations. When she did, she was glad for the family God had given her.

WINDFALL INHERITANCE

The ephemeral day is all our treasure—
Only now does the wild wind blow;
Only now the clean cloud-laundry pile up white in the sky.
Only now the lilacs tumble their scented beards upon the breeze.
Paupers indeed if all our thoughts are of yesterday or tomorrow,
We beggar ourselves, squandering fortunes freely bestowed upon us.

I have lived in pain, and I know that today's pain is bearable,
Couched as it is in terms of robins and violets.
It is yesterday's and tomorrow's woes which crush us.
You are free to disagree, it's your concern.
But I will gorge myself upon today,
Served up upon the silver air of spring.
I will revel in the wilderness of green untrammeled
No matter how many houses hem it in.
I will sate myself with fire of tulips,
Adorn myself with diamonds in eyes that behold love.
I will share your tears and make you laugh today,
Riches beyond compare!
And if tomorrow's hot breath or yesterday's chill fingers shall touch me,
I shall give them a piece of today to pay their bills.

ELEVENTH DAY

Perfect Day

Above all, love each other deeply,
because love covers over a multitude of sins.
1 Peter 4:8

When my daughter graduated from high school, I pulled her memory box out from the back of my closet and shared a couple of hours with her, saying good-bye to her childhood. Especially the last two years in high school were filled with battles over chores, homework, dating, curfews, rules. Whatever respect I had for myself as a parent by then was quite tattered.

We pulled up old photos, homemade valentines, school projects, report cards, notes to each other, birthday cards, and her drawings and artwork from the bottom of the overflowing box. We remembered how we had moved to Illinois from California when she was two, with only a suitcase apiece, borrowing a carpet and a floor pillow to be our living room. We remembered the evenings we spent after work playing there. I used to take a clean watercolor brush and brush her face with it, pretending I was painting her into my picture.

There were so many good things in that box that the lid wouldn't stay on. We had both forgotten there had been so much love between us. She cried as we closed up the box, confiding that it had been so good to be taken care of, and it was so scary now to be going away to college.

I held her and wept myself, in gratitude that it hadn't been all pain and struggle, that there were scenes of love we both could take into the future for comfort. I wept in gratitude for the little girl who had been such a wonder and a joy to me, who had so mysteriously changed into this independent young woman.

I wept, in short, like any other parent of any other grown-up child. Our lives had not been less loving or more painful because I was a single parent. God had provided graciously for both of us. Neither she nor I had been punished for being a single-parent family. We had only been helped and healed.

So many things have been said in the church to the contrary! The truth, however, is that if we are willing, God will fill our lives with love no matter what our circumstances, past sins, the weight of our grief over losses. We have only to open our arms to receive. God longs to pour love into the world: it's the only thing that can change any of the suffering or sin. We were given that, thank God, pressed down and running over the sides of the box.

PERFECT DAY

With a gentle hand,
The wind combs the hill's glossy green flank.
She glows in response,
"I love you."
The shimmering reeds swoon
Under the ardent caress of sun and wind,
"Water, wind, sun, earth, and air,
"I love you."
The sunflowers tilt back their heads to say,
"I love you"; so also sings the sycamore.
The cornstalks in precise military formation chorus,
"We, too."
Flocking above the fields of flowers,
The newborn monarchs setting sail
Astonished, gasp, "I love you."
The pond, alive with every shade of leaf and fin and wing,
Opens her arms to the sky, "See how beautiful you are."
The poplars cast their cooling shade over somnolent cows who mumble, "Yes."
Sheep drift like cloud shadows across the meadow,
Munching their agreement,
"Amen, amen."
The sun slips lower now,
As I find refuge in your holy presence
And add my voice
To the chant of millions,
"Good night, good night,
"I love you."

Go Ahead, Ask Me

Though my father and mother forsake me, the Lord will receive me.
Psalm 27:10

Much has been said about the father-love of God. But I was reminded by a man whose mother died when he was young that God provides mother-love, too. Isaiah 66 and Psalm 131, among many other Scriptures, speak of this.

My personal favorite is Jesus' declaration to Nicodemus (John 3:6), "Spirit gives birth to spirit." I realize that Jesus is saying the Holy Spirit is our mother, who gives us birth. Just like a good mother does, the Holy Spirit prays for us, "with groans that words cannot express" (Rom. 8:26) when in our weakness we do not even know what to pray.

How else can we hope, as single parents (or as imperfect parents, for that matter), that God will make up for our deficiencies? So many of us have hurting children inside our memories who long for the blessing of the father or the love of the mother which for some reason was denied. How will these deficiencies ever be made up?

One of the mistakes made in my community was to designate individuals to be surrogate mothers or fathers for specific children (or adults). It seemed a great idea. But the mistake was to think that the children would therefore not feel the loss of the missing parent's blessing—and would not experience loss afresh when the surrogates moved on.

Now, years later, many of our Reba folks are adoptive parents who know the time will come when their children grow up and want to know about their "real" (biological) parents. Many of our adults are still trying to deal with their hurting inner children, in spite of years of effort by counselors to heal them. We have now learned that, while God does make up for the deficiencies of our parents (and of our culture), God is sovereign in who gets chosen for these remedial tasks.

An instructive meditation for me was to go over my life year by year, beginning at birth, and make a list of all the people who had shown me real love and how they had done so. It was healing to realize that when my parents were overwhelmed with their responsibilities and could not meet my need for love, God was selecting others—anyone at hand, really —like my grandmother, aunts and uncles, school friends, and even neighbors and a teacher or two, to supply my need.

My problem was that I had been looking for that supply from two specific individuals, and when there was a lack there, as is inevitable, I felt unloved. Amazingly enough, when I saw that God had been supplying my need through others I had not recognized, I was healed even thirty years later of that basic hurt.

GO AHEAD, ASK ME

God asked me, "What do you want for Christmas?"
"Can it be anything?"
"Anything."
I thought a long time.
"A perfect fall day?"
"I've already given you that."
It was true. A long life?
I didn't know if I would really need that.
Happiness? I'd already been given that, too.
I imagined myself famous. Disappointing.
What about rich? I thought of feeding hungry kids,
But soon the money was all gone, and they were hungry again.
"Bless my daughter's life."
"I've already done that, too."
"Justice for the poor?"
"That is something you give me," God pointed out.
"Rescue the planet from destruction?"
"I gave you that the first Christmas."
"World peace?"
"Ditto."
"Do you know what I really want?" I asked.
"Try me," God said.
"I want to see Jesus."
And God laughed out loud, arms held wide, saying,
"I thought you'd never ask."

I also learned that when I felt rejected, unloved, unwanted, or a burden to those around me, the wounding thing about that experience was to agree that this must be the truth about me. I learned instead to take care of myself, to be gentle as a mother to myself or as encouraging as a father who believes in his child's ability to grow when I needed that, knowing that was how God wanted me (and everyone) to be treated. God called that "receiving Jesus' love."

Now I know this: even when there's no one immediately at hand for God to use, I can receive God's love—God's best for me.

I realize that this is God's goal for us and our children—that we grow up—and this happens when we realize we are beloved, precious beyond measure, to the Ruler of the universe.

Orphan

I will not leave you as orphans; I will come to you.
John 14:18

Jesus had a lot to say about the necessity of loss (see Matt. 18; Luke 17). Jesus knew this world is full of pain caused by sin—our own and others'. Imagine the dismay of the disciples when they learn Jesus—the best friend, counselor, healer, and teacher they have ever had—is leaving them.

We single parents feel this pain most keenly for our children. The virgin Mary had this prophecy spoken about her: "And a sword will pierce your own heart also." It feels to me a lot like a sword in the heart whenever I touch the pain of children who are missing the absent parent. There is something inside all of us, I believe, which feels this pain, no matter whether our parents were wonderful or awful to us. It is one of those "unspeakable longings" the Bible talks about.

How do you explain to a two-year-old that God will come to us? (Two is not too early to feel such longing!) Many are the words that can be said, but words alone will not heal this pain. These are the times for touching, reaching out, for comforting arms to be spread to hold the hurting one, often without words. (Eighteen or eighty is not too old to need this.)

It is so important to accept the child's pain in all its heaviness, not to minimize or rationalize it away, not to condemn such feelings as unfaithful or unworthy. Pain is pain and hurts everybody. Jesus says pain is even necessary. It is a part of our assignment on this planet to learn compassion through suffering.

We parents teach compassion by offering comfort and explaining that pain is part of life. It does much harm to blame the absent parent, because the child identifies as the product of both and so feels there must be something wrong with her if one parent is "bad." If the absent parent is of another race or faith, it is important for the child to be exposed to that part of his heritage, so something good is received from the absent parent.

Our pain at the loss of a partner can be as great as the child's at the loss of a parent. We need to be gentle and compassionate with ourselves as well, making allowances for grieving and accepting the overtures of supporters. They are agents of the Holy Spirit, sent to comfort us. We need to go to God in prayer, too, asking to be held and loved. Jesus has promised not to leave us orphans.

ORPHAN

I cannot name this restless longing.
I only know that, like an orphan,
I hunt the mysteriously vanished
Father and Mother of my soul.

Lost in the universe's train station,
I look up and see only the ceiling;
Out, and see many crowded paths,
But I find no one to meet me.

Until at last in despair of despairing
I draw all myself within
A central core of life and mystery,
Breath and body, and find you there, Jesus.

We laugh. It was an excellent hiding place.
And I cry a little, too: sheer relief.
The game had lasted nearly too long.
So you hold me and comfort me, till I sleep.

Water

For our light and momentary troubles are achieving for us
an eternal glory that far outweighs them all.
2 Corinthians 4:17

I was reflecting yesterday on the story of Gabriel's announcement to Zechariah. Because I knew how John would die, I felt dread for his parents. The story speaks only of joy and delight that this son will bring, unlike Mary's story, which mentions a sword piercing her own heart.

How many times have I felt that pain for my daughter—when a friend repeatedly destroyed her "Daddy" doll, saying my daughter had no daddy; when her father answered her hopeful letter months late with cold comfort; when her teacher criticized her in front of the class; when she lost her job; when her boyfriend dumped her.

We cannot help feeling this pain—it is a part of our humanity to wince when someone else is hurt. Yet sometimes I and other parents have gone further and tried to feel our children's pain *for* them to shield them. Not only does this add unnecessary heaviness to our own burdens, it does nothing to lessen their pain. To try to lighten the pain of others by feeling it yourself is to have more faith in your own strength and ability to learn than in theirs. It also is not very accurate: I can feel something as a much bigger issue than it is to my daughter. It's an excess of sympathy which actually gives the other person more to deal with than before.

When I became pregnant, my mother was devastated. She remarked, "This will *kill* your grandmother!"

I loved my grandmother. Now to my shame I had to add the guilt of causing her grief.

A bitterly grieving friend, a single parent for many years, was consoled by her friends when her teen-age daughter became pregnant. But one friend did more good than all the rest when she refused to treat it as a tragedy. "A child is *always* a gift from God," she stated.

When my mother died suddenly at age fifty-one, a friend welcomed me to her house to cry and tell her all about my mother for hours and hours. She later gave me a plaque which read, "Weeping may last for a night, but joy cometh in the morning" (Ps. 30:5).

We dare not carry our children's pain—it is meant to be used for their good. We can feel sad when they do—but not sadder than they feel. We can do for them which they cannot do for themselves: have faith that God is at work to transform all our pain into an eternal triumph of love.

WATER

I had this discussion with my daughter
As my mother had with me:
Is the glass of water
Half full or half empty?

It's a matter of choice, I said,
But I was wrong.
That glass is full.
Where the water stops, the air begins,
And while we last only a little
Without the water of life,
We live not at all
Without the breath of it.

All is gift.
Even the half that seems empty
Is brimming over with good.
So how then death,
And my daughter's pain
That her father rejects her?
Are they but the empty-seeming
Breath from which we draw life?
They the pain from which we draw
The comfort of the loving Spirit
And an assurance of the ever-presence
Of the strong Companion
Who once was likened
To the unseen breath that moves the trees?

So I believe; so I believe,
Who know that whisper,
The certainty of that promise:
The glass is full.
And how shall I tell it to you in your grief?
Let me touch you.
Let me breathe upon your face.
Like the face of the waters of chaos,
Receive the Holy Spirit.

The Argument from Necessity for the Incarnation of God

Although he was a son, he learned obedience from what he suffered and, once made perfect, he became the source of eternal salvation for all who obey him.
Hebrews 5:8-9

"I hate you!" Oh, how familiar those words are to many parents! As the mother of an only daughter, they were perhaps more familiar to me than most. She and I fought a lot. It worried me, so we went to family counselors.

They all said, "It's normal, especially in your situation."

Every child, it seems, must struggle to dissociate from the parent and become a separate individual. For most parents, this feels like rejection, like being out of control. For two people who were as close as we inevitably were, who had no one else except each other, it was terrifying. The independence my daughter so desperately desired meant for both of us the weakening of a bond to the most important person in our lives.

The more we tried to let go of each other, the more tightly entwined we became, although this was not so obvious to us. Each of us developed an intense focus on the problems in the relationship. She felt angry because she could not do what she wanted to do when she wanted to do it. I felt anxious for her safety, guilty because I was angry at her for the way she talked to me, and ashamed that I had doubtless created the problems we were now battling. Talk about a lose-lose situation!

We continued in counseling without much success. The struggle wore on for years. I noticed as she made and discarded friends that she was looking for as intense a focus with someone else as she had with me. I could see this was not going to work—but could only encourage her to keep looking for friends.

When she was fourteen, I made a friend who became important to me. This forced my daughter increasingly to look elsewhere for intimacy, as my time was more and more taken up. I felt guilt for this *and* awareness that it was right for my daughter to look elsewhere. It felt like an abandonment to both of us.

She fought my new friend with every weapon at her disposal, principally my guilt. I learned to set limits, but it grieved me to see her so lonely. I worried about the new friends she had made, who seemed to be careless of her feelings, her well-being, even her self-esteem. But who was I to complain? I had forced her into it. Even today this struggle rages in less intense form.

The years have taught me this: God is with us. We will not be abandoned. In the end we will be healed. My commission is to love this daughter, and the most important way to love her right now is to believe in her God-given ability to learn and grow; to respect her choices as necessary ingredients for that growth, even when they hurt her. One other crucial thing: I must believe God is powerfully at work to heal and save her, even though this work is hidden so deep in her life I cannot see it.

God promised me it would be all right; I believe it. I also pray the father's prayer: "Help my unbelief!" God only asks, "Can you be patient while she tries to find her heavenly Parent?"

THE ARGUMENT FROM NECESSITY
FOR THE INCARNATION OF GOD

Lost and gone all savage
From longing for home,
How could we understand,
Unless a person came for us?

Insane from the need for a touch
That regards while freeing us,
How could we trust again,
Unless a person was sent for us?

Blind with grief for all we have lost,
How could words or principles or cosmic forces
Ever meet, embrace, or comfort us,
Unless a person arrived for us?

He came, asking nothing,
Offering everything,
And in our rage and pain
We killed him.

In his death he fully shared
Our homelessness,
The cause of our madness.
Yet his life, sprouting again
In the darkness of the tomb
Now opens out again,
Our way home.

He was sent for us,
And how shall we not now go with him?
Bone of our bone,
Flesh of our flesh,
Passion of our passion,
Our trust in him flowers under his touch,
And we shall indeed with him
Win home.

Great Expectations

*"For I know the plans I have for you," declares the Lord, "plans to pros-
per you and not to harm you, plans to give you hope and a future."*
Jeremiah 29:11

Possibly the most important lesson I've had in parenting is con-
tained in the above verse. It is set in the time of the destruction of Jerusalem and the exile, the nadir of Hebrew history.

Yet God gives hope. God once said to me, "You keep dreading disaster, imagining the worst. You're going to be awfully disappointed. I
only have good for you."

I laughed then, and I laugh still, because it's true. But I only gradually
learned how important it is to communicate this to our children. Listen to
what I used to say to my daughter.

"If you keep on like this, you'll never . . ."

"If you don't be careful, you'll end up . . ."

"Do this (or don't do this) or else . . . will happen."

You might say these are all threats. I was motivated by anxiety for her
welfare, not punitive anger. It has the same effect, unfortunately. The
child becomes anxious, not believing or trusting that God has given or
will give him or her enough to cope with whatever comes.

That is not what God intended. We are here for a purpose. God
wants us to fulfill it and offers the resources of heaven to see that we do.
God is *for* us, not against us. God plans to give us the kingdom of love
(Luke 12:32); we can share that good news with our children.

"I think you can do it. Let's see how . . ."

"If this doesn't work out, you can choose a different way."

"What can we salvage from this experience?"

"God never closes a door without opening a window."

"I wonder what God wants to make from this?"

In the words of a popular saying, "Lord, there's nothing that can happen today that together you and I can't handle."

These are the words of life.

53

GREATEXPECTATIONS

My heart is not proud, O Lord,
my eyes are not haughty;
I do not concern myself with great matters
or things too wonderful for me.
But I have stilled and quieted my soul;
like a weaned child with its mother,
like a weaned child is my soul within me.
O Israel, put your hope in the Lord
both now and forevermore.
—Psalm 131

As Jacob limped from Peniel,
He felt no pain,
His heart instead leaping at the blessing.

Forty years he schemed for Isaac's blessing;
Twenty years more he labored for Laban,
Neither stealing nor earning what he sought.

In desperation, he wrestled with a mighty stranger,
Receiving at dawn what he had always owned
But never believed in—his blessing.

Isn't that our trouble, too?
God wants to bless us—
All lives reveal this truth—
And bless he will,
Pouring down rivers of blessing,
New life, new hope, new love
Spilling over onto all those standing by.
And just as he did at Cana,
God saves the best till last.

No striving of ours will change it:
Our God is a God of celebrations
Of life, a God of glorious blessing.
Ours is to wait in hope, believing.
"O Israel, put your hope in the Lord, both
now and forevermore."

God Has Gotten a Very Bad Name

*I am still confident of this: I will see the goodness
of the Lord in the land of the living.*
Psalm 27:13

My friend's husband left her and their three children for another woman more than twenty years ago. It shattered her. Painfully, and as we sing here, "leaning on the Lord," she rebuilt her life, raising her children alone. Her grandchildren now live in another state, and my friend lives downstairs, caring for her wonderful mother. This year she learned that her daughter and son-in-law were divorcing. This was almost more than she could take. First she and now her daughter, first her children and now her grandchildren must walk this stony path.

My heart ached for her and for the children. Her twelve-year-old grandson phoned last night to tell his great-grandma, "I'm depressed. There's nothing wrong with school or football; it's just me that isn't right."

Why, God? Why must the children suffer so, taking upon themselves the sins and failures of their parents? Surely the ocean of sorrow needs no fresh contributions? My friend's mother says, "I feel so bad for him. We didn't do this in my time. We just hung in there with whatever was wrong."

Yet the children were living in fear of the ferocious arguments and hurtful words flying around their heads. My friend says she learned from her social work training that, except in the case of very young children, they often do as well or better living with only one parent than with two parents who do not cooperate.

So with heavy hearts, she and her mother helped move the mother and children into a new home. Can we trust in God's care? We all are living proof. Someone once said, "God writes straight with crooked lines." So he does. We wish we could get our lines straightened out so God wouldn't have to—and we work at that, too. We hope that our children can learn from our mistakes, and cry when they have to learn from their own.

God doesn't give up. God keeps working with us. For that we are so grateful. God's hope for us is without bounds. We are invited to hope with him—God has promised us a new heaven and a new earth.

GOD HAS GOTTEN A VERY BAD NAME

God has gotten a very bad name for himself.
I don't know how he did it.
First we got mad,
Then we slandered and hit and hurt and killed each other,
And then we blamed God for the lousy way
He let us be who we are.
Meanwhile, he was busy cleaning up the mess.
I guess that's why the word got around so fast.
He was too busy stanching the blood
To defend himself.
Besides, God isn't very good at defending himself.
I mean, what would he say?
"It's because I love you that I don't chain you all to the wall"?

He sent his Son to try to explain himself to us—
All that immensity of passion and touch.
But we gave him a bad name, too,
And hustled him off to die.
Would have done the same to God
If we could.

Why,
When the Christ-mass
Weeps Sons and suns, stars of fire
And angels of light,
And bushes of straw and warm oxen-breath,
Why is our response
Herod's soldiers' bloody swords
And piles of infant dead?

Oh, but it is not for us all,
Hand-held, coddled, mewling brats,
Demanding more, and proof, and me.
Not for Herod, nor Pilate, nor Caiaphas.
It is for them, and anyone who will,
Face forward, faith-filled, simple,
Measuring the black dark of the road ahead
With foot-tread and heart-beat,
Minds a bare, single thread taut as a harp-string,
Breath held and eyes caught by a hope too sharp for name:
For Mary, Joseph, shepherds, magi,
The pilgrim folk,
Marching off the edge of black abyss
Into the future of God.
It is for them he waits
And offers up himself
In the blood-red dark,
Which yet holds hope of morning.
He may not understand the name
We have given him,
But he thinks no shame of it—
Only a single prayer:
May a Salome become a Mary?
Let it be so.

Dayenu

*Has not God chosen those who are poor in the eyes of the world
to be rich in faith and to inherit the kingdom
he promised those who love him?*
James 2:5

My daughter asked me one Christmas, "Mom, are we poor?" I was surprised. We live in a Christian community where we share all our income. The personal allowance we receive is limited but not stingy. The reality for many single parents is not so comfortable. In the United States, 41 percent of single mothers and one-third of single fathers and their children live below the poverty level, according to one study (Aaron Bernstein, "When the Only Parent Is Daddy," *Business Week*, Nov. 23, 1992, p. 127).

Many single parents in our city share apartments with other single parents, while their mothers care for the grandchildren. After an unexpected surgery which wiped out our savings, my daughter and I were on welfare. This was humiliating but taught me what people who are poor have to go through. Heaven help them if they cannot fill out forms or have to wait for weeks for errors in paperwork to be straightened out.

The economics of single parenting are daunting. Most single mothers and fathers must work full-time. Courts are slow to demand child support payments from noncustodial mothers, and it is often easy for noncustodial fathers to avoid paying child support.

Some noncustodial fathers are raising other families or don't get enough pay to support two households. If single parents work full-time, there are years they need to pay for full-time child care or after-school care. This can take up to half of a parent's salary. If the job offers no health benefits or health insurance is not affordable, one small illness or injury can wipe the family out.

If you have found a church which practices a pure religion (James

1:27), rejoice! If you haven't, see if you can cooperate with others in your situation. When we share, there always seems to be more than enough to go around. *Dayenu!* (it is enough).

I have found, too, that needs are smaller than we believe. We have had to go without money for anything except food, utilities, and rent for months at a time. But we often laugh about not really noticing we weren't buying anything—we were too busy having fun and enjoying our friends.

If we really needed something (even sometimes if we only badly wanted it), someone would often offer it unasked—a living room rug, couch, vacuum cleaner, bed, snowsuit, child's shoes. Our church maintains the "Pick" room. It is staffed every Saturday morning by volunteers so people can bring unwanted items to share with others. We have to reach beyond our neighborhood to bring in enough people to take away all the donations! When we share our bread, God multiplies it.

DAYENU

Oh, Lord, the beautiful sun rising in my window,
Dayenu! It is enough! But you add
Bread baked by my neighbor,
Yeasty, warm, and soft. Dayenu!

And you add a hug from my grown-up daughter
Who now says, "I don't get that often enough,"
And a wide and welcoming smile from her baby.
Dayenu! And then you add a phone call
In the middle of the day from someone who says,
"I love you." Dayenu!

My body is healthy enough to cook and clean,
And I can walk to work through crisp, red leaves,
And I can see and smell and taste the coming fall.
Dayenu! In Africa, I am told,
Riches are measured in friendships;
So in Africa I would be considered wealthy.
Dayenu! But to this you add
Your own love, your own friendship.

I stand in piles of tumbled treasure
And watch for one of your friends
To need something. Dayenu!

The Eden Tree

And a little child will lead them.
Isaiah 11:6

In single-parent families, children are often drawn into the adult responsibilities of the absent parent. We are encouraged *not* to say to our sons or daughters, "You're the man of the house now," or "You'll have to do the things your mother used to." Even if we don't say these things, which can overwhelm a child, single-parent families tend to involve children more in decision making than most two-parent families do.

My friend Adrienne's mother was a single parent when Adrienne and her brother were teenagers. I smiled when she told me how they had carefully looked over would-be suitors for their mother's attention and scared off those who didn't seem "good enough for her."

Children often do feel responsible to take care of the one parent they have left. It was a big relief for my daughter when she could look forward to leaving home without worrying about my being devastated by the loss.

Some of this is normal and can be good for children, giving them maturity and wisdom beyond their years. But none of us wants something like what happened to Carole, who fell apart when her fifteen-year-old daughter got pregnant and left home. Her daughter had been her sole emotional caretaker, and Carole went into prolonged mental illness.

There are several points to keep in mind when considering children's responsibility. One is that the Lord, not the child, should fill the missing parent's role. Children will naturally be more involved in decision making but should not have to carry the responsibilities of parenting themselves—or their parent. Nor should they feel responsible to keep peace between separated parents or to take sides. The single parent's most powerful resource is prayer. We can ask for anything according to God's will—which is love—and we will receive.

Second, the parent should be sure the child knows he or she is not responsible when the parent feels angry, sad, depressed. I was depressed a lot during my daughter's youth, and she would often try to comfort me. I had to tell her my sadness wasn't about her and that I was trying my best to deal with my feelings so I could be a good mom.

Third, parents must take care of themselves. Whether that involves therapy, prayer, or spending time with friends or family, we need to do it so our children will know it is not their responsibility. It is also good for them to learn by example how adults take care of themselves. They will be less apt in later life to hunt someone to take care of them, or worse, to hunt for someone who needs taking care of as their parent did.

THE EDEN TREE

I used to love to run outdoors,
Play football, climb trees.
There was one tree in particular
Which presided over all our games.
It could have been the original Eden tree, for all I knew.
It was huge; and in its shadow, we played soldiers.
We climbed it when we were big enough, and safely it held us.
It formed a boundary for all our play for years and years,
Holding conversation with the wind, watching us grow,
And making a glory of the sun when it shone.
I love that Eden tree,
And in my mind it stands as beacon,
Tall and protecting, marking the beauty of my growing up.

When last I visited the Eden tree,
Someone had chopped most of it away.
Yet, much reduced, new branches had grown from its sides,
And still it made a glory of the sun.
It laughed at my dismay, and letting its leaves be tossed by the wind,
It cried, "I am the Eden tree! I live!"

Tears catch in my throat as I remember
How you stood over my childhood like that tree,
Tall and protecting, enduring storm after storm,
Lightning, hail, and snow, and many a long drought.
You suffered much that I might grow well;
And I barely noticed, engrossed in my games,
How you formed the boundary that shaped my life.
I owe to God my faith, yet I owe it as much to you,
Who pointed my steps in the right direction.
I owe to God my life and health,
Yet I owe them as much to you who guarded them.

I came back to say thank you to the Eden tree
And found it full of light and life,
Laughing with the wind though much had been taken away.
I come back now to say thank you to you,
And to say that in my mind I will always dwell in your shadow,
Though I am grown; and that, though far away, my roots drink
From the same soil you marked out for me,
Nurtured by the same love of God which feeds you.

Parents of mine, together you form my Eden tree.
No matter what time may take away,
It cannot take away this: I love you.

The Spirit Prays

Rejoice in the Lord always. . . . Do not be anxious about anything, but in everything, by prayer and petition, with thanksgiving, present your requests to God. And the peace of God, which transcends all under- standing, will guard your hearts and your minds in Christ Jesus.
Philippians 4:4, 5-7

A leader in the church came up to me one day to tell me what he thought of my raising a child alone. He said, "I hope your daughter al- ways feels the pain of what she is missing by not having a father."

I think he was trying to tell me he thought fathers are essential in a child's life; that my child was really missing out; and that if I did not keep telling her what she was missing, she might not know.

I told him, "Dwelling on what we don't have is a dead-end street."

Our materialistic culture survives by constantly showing us what we lack. It's no accident that the people depicted in the movies appear richer and richer. Crime spreads as the gap between rich and poor grows. Single folks envy the married. Even women who have been married disastrously still dream that the right man will save them from loneliness and be a fa- ther to their children. God points us in a different direction.

My daughter was unhappy one day, "I'm bored," she moaned. "I'm depressed. There's nothing to do, and I don't have any friends."

I was inspired to give her an assignment. "Write down twenty things in your life you're thankful for," I told her.

She griped for a while, then settled down to write for thirty minutes. She was transformed when she finished. Cheerful and busy, she soon found something enjoyable to do.

The Lord told me once that thankfulness is the key to get out of the prison of depression. I'm tempted to believe it is a key that works in any prison. If you want to be blessed, try sitting down with your children and thanking God for the good things.

Thank God for the wonderful qualities of the parent who is not with you, those same qualities now present in your children. Thank God for the time you had with that person, however brief. Thank God for the wonderful memories you have of people with whom you've shared love, even if they are now deceased.

Scripture tell us to thank God in everything. Be creative. You can do it. Instead of discontent and shame, you will have the peace of God. I have learned to thank God for what he has done in the past when I feel he is far away. Soon I begin to see that he is doing those same things in the present; I haven't been paying attention.

We're teaching our children something valuable without measure when we do this, and we're forming their self-esteem. We're not training them to think of themselves as motherless or fatherless children or to think of their lives as deficient. Rather, we're teaching them that they're beloved children of a heavenly Father and a heavenly Mother who gives them everything they need.

THE SPIRIT PRAYS

A pink redbud
Yellow dandelion
My soul embraces these.
A gray river pebble
The Colorado Rockies
A stripy cat
The comic rhinoceros
My soul reaches to these also.
My mother watches me play
And speaks from heaven,
"My child, you are my delight."
In the silence of pines
The roar of the ocean
In the eyes, arms, and voices
Of all those who love me, old and young,
Living or dead,
In the companionship
Between husband and wife that needs no speech,
My beloved leans out heaven's window
To say, "You whom I have made, I bless you."

In the sadness of a city's burning,
Too slow in learning the ways of love,
In the grief of mothers
Who have lost their children
To U.S. bombs or street gangs or simple hunger,
My soul reaches out to touch my Savior
Who knows
And heals, I know not how, though I know its cost.
From the depths of this mystery,
He calls me, "Be alive.
"Be so full of life. Be love.
"Be my love." And somehow,
My soul fills with Christ, and I do.

Unless You Become as a Little Child

Whatever is true, whatever is noble, whatever is right, whatever is pure,
whatever is lovely, whatever is admirable—if anything is excellent
or praiseworthy—think about such things. Whatever you have
learned or received or heard from me, or seen in me—
put it into practice. And the God
of peace will be with you.
Philippians 4:8-9

How many of us know TV is a lousy babysitter? Good, everyone raised their hands. How many of us use it anyway? Not so good.

I found it especially tempting as a single parent to use TV as an after-school program. I found seductive the reasoning that we can choose what we watch and weed out the bad programs. There was also the folk wisdom that if they don't watch it at our house, they'll go to someone else's house; better to have it in our own home, where we can process it with them.

Now that I have lived for several years without TV, I feel differently. If there were one thing I could change (well, maybe two) about my parenting days, the second would be no television!

Whether we like it or not, children *do* graduate from *Mr. Rogers* and *Sesame Street*. They do learn to change that channel. Aside from the torrent of violent, abusive, vile, immoral, and blasphemous offerings which spews from the set, the television is the primary inculcator of greed and selfishness in our society. Advertising teaches our children to focus on what they don't have, on their wants, not on others' needs.

To counter every lie, every distortion, point out every seductive portrayal of immorality is impossible. We end up having time to deal with only the most outrageous instances and leaving an immense pile of bad input unsorted. For single parents particularly, since our time with our children is usually so limited, television should be seen not as babysitter but as a kidnapper sending ransom notes.

Television also teaches us to suspend judgment and wait passively to be entertained by whatever someone else chooses to offer us. "I don't want to spend my life in a series of mild entertainments," I once heard a wise woman say. I don't want to teach my children this is desirable either.

Active play, creative play, imaginative play, playing with other children, sharing stories of family and work or from the Bible, entertaining guests, becoming aware of the needs of others (especially the poor), sports, music, dance, scouting, dressing up in old clothes and putting on plays, writing letters to a sponsored child, learning how to work, caring for a pet or a younger child, learning about other cultures, studying almost anything, sharing family worship, praying with a parent for friends and family, and even just plain daydreaming are infinitely more valuable activities for children. And that's only the start of a long list.

If our children are doing these things at home, all the kids in the neighborhood will be coming to our house to get in on the fun.

UNLESS YOU BECOME AS A LITTLE CHILD

What if all the cars in the world broke down?
And all the electricity stopped flowing?
Would that be the end
Of childhood as we know it?
No TVs, no computers, no video games,
No shopping malls, no adult agendas for any child to address?

Would children still play tick-tack-toe
And old maid and jacks and marbles and jump rope?
Would they still sing "Jesus Loves Me,"
And recite "Miss Mary Mack" and tell knock-knock jokes?
Would they still tell stories to each other and play school
And put on old clothes and make up plays for adults to watch?

And if the TVs weren't constantly scaring everybody to death,
And making everybody mad and wishing for more of everything,
Would children still play in the parks and the yards and on porches?
I bet they might.

Let's try it and see if I'm right.

Harvest Time

I am the vine; you are the branches. If [you] remain in me and I in [you], [you] will bear much fruit; apart from me you can do nothing.
John 15:5

For years I kept a poem tacked to my kitchen wall which reminded me that the days were speeding by and soon my daughter would be grown. I counted each day precious, but that did not keep me from feeling shocked and devastated when I looked into her empty room the day after she left for college.

I had a busy and happy life but I felt as if the floor had dropped out without warning. I had known she would leave. Why was I so shocked? During the next month, I wandered into her room nearly every day to look for something she had left behind which she might need or want. I packed several boxes and mailed them to her. Whenever I was at home, I felt at loose ends, wishing there was something I could still do for her.

This, I learned, is letting go. I could never have done it without Jesus' help. He began to teach me there was still something I could do: release her into his care, praying for his blessing for her. At times I felt she had left before I finished my job. There must be something more I could or should be doing for her. When she would call and tell me how deeply she was struggling, I was sure of it.

But the Lord said, "Let her go to me. This job has always been mine. Your part is finished."

I pleaded, "But there's so much I did wrong, so much I neglected, so much I failed to teach her, so much bitterness between us."

One day God said, "Do you know why I am pleased with what you have done, even though you aren't? Because after everything that has been said and done, you are still aiming at loving her. Loving her now means letting me take over."

Gradually it became easier, although never easy. I saw that our children are like the fruit on the branches. The fruit must be cast for the seed to sprout. From the vine has come everything needed for the seed to grow. But only from the branch can come the release that allows the seed to be planted. I had to trust that the Vine had provided everything necessary for life—for me and for my daughter.

Letting go is the hardest thing I ever did. Letting God is the best.

HARVEST TIME

As the farmer gathers in the hay,
Piling golden bales roof-high in the barn,
And stores potatoes and apples
In the cool, dry cellar,
Thankful to God and the weather—
So it is with me, my daughter,
As you say goodbye to us,
Looking back with a wave
And a tentative smile
As you enter a new door,
To be greeted by unfamiliar faces.

It was hard work, yes,
These seventeen years,
The daily-paid mortgage of love.
But as with the farmer
Who has labored over many a crop that failed
From too much rain or not enough,
Or gophers or rabbits or deer or birds
Or insects or hail or tornadoes or fire,
Or timing just plain gone wrong,
Who sees this year, this crop
Is safe in the barn,
So it is with me, my daughter,
As you leave me to learn
Other lessons from other teachers.
You are young and beautiful and perfect;
We have made it, you and we,
The entire village of folk who have cared for you
From birth to now, by the grace of God.
And we celebrate and rejoice
And grieve a little for the passing
Of a perfect season.

Labor of Love

My yoke is easy and my burden is light.

Matthew 11:30

Recently I learned that my nineteen-year-old daughter is pregnant. Ordinarily this would be cause for rejoicing. But she is single. I was filled with grief. And guilt. I felt I was to blame.

She of all people should know how difficult and painful it will be for the child, let alone for herself. She is sad, too. I cried and cried for her, for what she has not yet learned, and for myself, for what I did not teach her, hard as I tried.

I felt such failure. I went to God, grieving and ashamed. "You are making it so hard for yourself," God replied. "She will be a good mother because she *had* a good mother. Just because once there were things you had not learned and now there remain things you have yet to learn does not mean you have failed. Learn what you need to learn, and go on. Your burden is too heavy unless you let me make it light. You are a good mother. I am proud of all you've learned so far."

I began to see the things I had missed: my daughter's courage in the face of rejection, her willingness to take responsibility for her choices, her patience and trust in looking for a job, her caring for her health for the baby's sake, her commitment to care for her child, even though she has to work very hard. There are many things about her of which God is proud. God's work in her so far is good. And I too am proud of her, of all she has learned so far.

LABOR OF LOVE

Single mom alone with child
Labor of love
Birthing—pain, sorrow, joy, and expectation—
"It's a girl!"
Labor of love.

Elspeth—God's promise—
Labor of love.

Provider, nurturer, caregiver;
Lover and teacher . . . endless sacrifices;
Labor of love.

Hopes, dreams, anxieties, and fears,
Labor of love

Letting go,
Labor of love.

Shattered dreams,
Grieving loss,
Labor of love.

Renewed hope,
"All shall be well,"
Labor of love.

Mother and child,
Forever and always,
Labor of love.

—Vincent Donoghue

I See You Hoping

As [one] thinks in [one's] heart, so is [that one.]
Proverbs 23:7, NKJV

I learned recently that the image we keep in our minds—of ourselves or of another person (or group)—is the template for what we create with God. This is important for parents to know.

The so-called Pygmalion studies should be required reading for parents. The researchers told teachers in advance whether students would perform well or poorly. Their random predictions, unrelated to the students' actual abilities, came true. The studies conclude that the most important factor in school performance is the teacher's expectation.

Today single parents are pushed to focus on problems. All sorts of things are blamed on single parenting, particularly juvenile crime. Some of the worst people I know have *two* parents who expect them to misbehave and who teach them they are bad. Morawetz and Walker (in *Brief Therapy with Single-Parent Families*, New York, 1984) found that family economics had more impact on family functioning than the presence of both parents! There is nothing about single parenting which guarantees poor outcomes for children. Even with poor parenting and low expectations, a poor outcome is not certain, because God has arranged it so that the parent is not the only influential person in any child's life.

I urge you not to buy into the vision of disaster. Here is an example of a different approach. Every summer since age fourteen, my daughter needed a job. Every summer I made a huge thing out of it. "If you don't get a job, blah, blah, blah."

The search was long and agonizing for both of us. The more anxious I became, the less intense her job search would be. The summer she was pregnant, getting a job was more important than ever. I vowed I would not nag her. I brought home ads, asked friends to keep an eye open for possibilities. I discovered she had written weeks before for an application for a counselor's job at a local day camp. She had not finished filling it out.

I knew she wanted this job. Why had she not applied? Normally I would have delivered an oration on getting things done on time so as not to miss out. But God stopped me. Instead I asked which question she was having trouble with. She replied that her previous experience seemed deficient.

I promised, "With all the experience you've had with childcare, I'll bet they'll grab you for this job as soon as you go in." I said more along the same lines—not *if* but *when* you go in.

She went in the next day and got the job. I could have worried still about her taking the responsibility to be on time or to show up every day. Instead, each day I thanked God before the fact for waking her up on time and getting her to work in a good frame of mind. Each day, though she was tired, she shared something that happened to cheer her. Then I rejoiced with her in the goodness of God's provision for her, which she knew all along would be there.

I SEE YOU HOPING

I see you hoping
And it eases my heart.
I was so worried.
My anxiety for you had squeezed
My feelings into a painfully tight little lump.
You were in such danger!

But you are expanded today,
Large in living, strong.
You have put out one bright, tentative blossom
Into the face of oncoming winter. Bravo!
I did well, did I not,
To entrust you into the hands of God?

The Pearl

But where sin increased, grace increased all the more, so that, just as sin reigned in death, so also grace might reign through righteousness to bring eternal life through Jesus Christ our Lord.
Romans 5:20

My friend Anne tells me there is an African-American phrase that goes, "God is my father, my mother, my sister, and my brother." She calls God the God of the gaps. She says there is a long list of things children need to thrive, but you only get in trouble if you think *you* are the list.

Scripture declares that God delights to *give* us the kingdom—the place where all needs are met and love rules supreme. In that kingdom, we are asked to meet the needs of people whom the world has thrown away—the poor—in love. Then all our own needs will be met. When we or our children feel like the people being thrown away, we are to open ourselves to God's love. When we are full, we are to give away the overflow.

God often fills in gaps through us, even when we have nothing of our own to give. Our being rejected, our sorrows and failures, our children's suffering make no sense if they are not occasions for love to abound—to us and through us. Yet they do make glorious sense if seen in this light.

Sometimes, when we are so weary we could drop—from sleepless nights, struggles with unmet needs, caring for children, trying to pay the bills, or praying with those whose needs are greater than our own—we need to be reminded why we do these things. We need to remember that the point is for love to abound!

In *Community and Growth*, Jean Vanier says that it is much easier to love the poor in groups far away than to love the ones you live with whose poverty is constantly pulling at you. My daughter struggles, just as I did before her, to come up with a loving response after being awakened by a crying baby for the fifth time in one night. These are the times we need to remember why we are trying to parent at all.

My friend Brucetta (also a single parent) says that if it weren't for parental love, we would all take our children back to the store, complaining that "this model leaks." Just before we head for the store, God wants us to remember: all of this is so love may increase.

THE PEARL

If my dying gives you life,
Makes you thrive under a safe heaven,
You whom I cherish,
Then death holds no terror
And torture no agony for me.
Freely I give you even my precious life,
You whom I love and long for,
My flesh and blood.
Oh, that you knew my joy
In giving you all that I have,
Emptying all my treasure for you!
I am the prodigal father
And you my beloved heir.
In your poverty, who have felt so little regard,
You cannot understand.
But I have come to make you rich,
To content you forever with my affection,
And you will have the priceless pearl:
To spend your life for love.

The Back Side of the Wave

All your waves and breakers have swept over me.
Psalm 42:7

This week I was talking to a friend who reminded me of what it is like on the back side of a wave. First you see a terrifying wall of water speeding toward you, then you feel it suck at you remorselessly. When you can't wait any longer, you take a deep breath, the enormous wall breaks on your head, and you kick, swimming up as hard as you can. As you open your eyes, you feel the back side of the wave lifting you, carrying you forward a little bit. You see the smooth curve of the unbroken water. The roar of the breaking wave is muffled behind you. It seems as peaceful and still as anything on earth. Then you feel the tug of the next wave beginning to draw you out farther.

On the back side of the wave, though you are tired, everything seems so gentle, easy. On the front side, you may have to struggle and kick; but on the back side, you are carried.

I am struck by how much single parenting, like other challenges of life, is like that. I remember how just at the point I thought, *Never again! I cannot take any more of this pain!* my daughter was born. When we went home from the hospital, it was several weeks before I had a night of unbroken sleep. I thought I would go mad. By the time I felt perhaps I could go on, year after year, without any sleep, she was sleeping peacefully through the night.

Each new challenge would stretch me nearly to the breaking point. Then it would recede, making everything seem so easy. There was nursing, teething, toilet training. There was pneumonia, then a glandular infection, then allergies. There was the welfare system to navigate. Before I knew it, there was school, homework (oh, dear Lord, all those term papers!), the challenge of making friends, all the hurts of immature relationships. Then came sleepovers. Then dates and broken curfews. Then her going away to college and all the worries of the things she tried there.

Then she got pregnant, and it seemed the end had come. But no, one last comber. She asked me to be her birth coach. I was terrified I would be no help at all or a big hindrance. It turned out to be the most wonderful experience. I was in awe of my daughter's riding those same frightening waves. She was so strong, even though her challenge was so much bigger than mine. And I was in awe of our Savior's courage in tackling the waves of this world as a puny human baby.

Finally I was dumbstruck at the courage of my granddaughter to choose life, to enter wholeheartedly and vigorously into the not-very-promising circumstances laid out for her and to begin smiling back the very first day. I was humbled by the power of life, and everything now seems possible.

THE BACK SIDE OF THE WAVE

The wall of water rushes toward me,
Foaming and rumbling.
Helpless, I am swept into it.
It lifts me high, higher till vertigo grips me,
And then it sucks me under,
Tons of water crashing on my unprotected head.

Gasping for air,
I glide down the smooth, broad back of the wave
Humped beneath me to break my fall.
The crash and roar are very faint here.
Weightless, I am towed up and over the back
Of the next wave and the next.
I roll onto my back and float in peace.

I know I will have to swim hard to reach the shore.
I know I will have to face many more waves
And use their force to carry me home.
But on the back of the wave is where I touch
The one whose ocean this is.
It's where I touch the solidity of the cross
That bore him up, up, up over the pain
And the loss and the defeat of all his hopes
Into the triumph of love.

Shoshanna Marie

Therefore, whoever humbles himself like this child is the greatest in the kingdom of heaven. And whoever welcomes a little child like this in my name welcomes me.
Matthew 18:4-5

I have good news for fathers. It is more amazing to witness a birth than give birth—at least it was for me. My granddaughter Shoshanna's birth was moderately difficult, revealing to me what an easy time I had had of it.

The nurse had told me to watch the heart monitor and notify them if it dipped below 100. I was sure nothing would happen, so I was astonished to glance over and see the numbers plummet to 83, then 63, then 57! And they stayed there. I probably didn't need the intercom—they could hear me in the hallway.

I never thought until then that people sometimes die during birth; it scared me badly. The baby kept trying to be born and slipping back. Soon we learned it was because she was facing the wrong way. Her mother was exhausted from hours of labor and was pleading for the doctor to help her.

I was focused on helping her remember to breathe, counting over and over again until she wanted to hit me. I counted as if it would save both their lives.

When she was finally delivered by forceps, I wept from sheer relief and a complex mix of other feelings, like being proud of her mother's strength and maturity in the crisis.

Then it hit me. *God* did this. Jesus took the risk of being born (and maybe dying in the process). He took the risk of not being wanted. He took the risk of disease and poverty and death that every human being takes. I kept saying to myself, "Wow! I never knew."

I was so impressed by Shoshanna's taking that risk and facing the added uncertainty of being the child of a single mother, that I vowed I would do whatever I could to help her thrive. She is strong and brave just to show up here, and she deserves all the love and help we can give her.

A few hours later, I held her while she studied me and her mother slept. Her eyes looked deep into mine. I knew I was looking at heaven—or the best reflection of it I will see on this earth. I promised her I would always love her, and she promised me she would live.

This is how God feels about every child. No matter what our limitations or our deficiencies, we owe them the best love we can muster—just because they had the courage and the faith to come here to be with us.

SHOSHANNA MARIE

I am in awe of you, of your mother.
I stood beside her through endless hours of pain,
Embarked upon the farthest journey we had ever taken.
Birth is such a terrifying passage.
I watched your heart beat slower and slower,
Shouted into the microphone,
Saw the medics' drawn faces as they ran into the room.
I hardly breathed myself.

When we started this journey
I assured myself nearly everybody makes it,
But as we traveled farther and farther from the shores of our accustomed conceits,
The unwanted thought occurred and clung unbidden: some don't.

As your mother struggled for your life and for hers, I prayed and waited.
Waiting and praying, knowing nothing,
I saw the doctor decide to help you out,
Witnessed your mother's courage and determination in battling the pain,
Saw your head come into view,
And then the medics came in like the last-minute cavalry,
And you were here, sudden, startling.
Unbelieving, I watched the doctor unwrap the cord from your neck,
Held my breath as he helped you breathe.
My heart hurt to hear your mother cry to hold you,
And she could not, not yet, they said.
Appalled, I watched them stitch her torn and bleeding body.

My tears could not be dammed—
I am so proud of you both and so amazed at you, too.
I see the glimmer of my tears reflected in the eyes of doctor and nurse.

Take pictures, your mother insists, so I do,
Stumbling over tubes and catheters, my eyes still blind with tears.
I see your grandpa's widest smile as you clutch his finger.

And now that anxious time is over,
And you lie in my lap while your mother sleeps,
Regarding me with eyes of silver that have the look of heaven in them,
Your tiny eyebrows tensed in concentration as you study me.
Then you sleep, your fists unclenched, and astonish me with brilliant smiles.
The nurse says angels are touching you, and my heart believes.
You have come from the creator of angels,
Your face like an open window to Christ's beauty, Christ's kingdom,
And I cannot help but adore when I look at you.

You are like him in that way:
You have come to help and bless us, blind as we are.
Welcome, little one, in the name and place of Jesus.

"Lord, Teach Us to Pray"

*But Jesus called the children to him and said, "Let the
little children come to me, and do not hinder them,
for the kingdom of God belongs to such as these."*
Luke 18:16

In my mind, the most important task of Christian parents is sharing their faith with their children. In a two-parent or extended family, the relationships between the adults can help model what love is. Practically no one exemplifies this ideal, however. And in a single-parent family, the model is broken. At Reba, many families have tried living in households. This can be a helpful addition, just as an extended family can be, but it is not a substitute for the love of the parents for each other or for the children.

You know the basics: tell them the stories about Jesus. Teach them to pray. Model Christian behavior and expect it of them as well. Don't scare them into belief. Avoid people who base their faith on fear and judgment.

An older friend remembers the good example of her mother saying the rosary with them at bedtime. They would all pile into bed. Their mother would often fall asleep in the middle of the recitation, but the experience was so loving and tender it made a lasting memory.

I always read stories of Jesus to my daughter, starting with the simplest books, even before she could understand. I prayed with her at bedtime and mealtimes. I taught her that God was her Father. Even though she couldn't touch him or see him, he was always there for her, loving her, listening to her.

I have great respect for God's power in response to the prayers of children, so we prayed when we were lost, when there were bad dreams or bad feelings, when I was sorry for what I had said or done, and once when a cherished rug was taken away. (My faith was tiny, but the rug was replaced within a week.) We listened to Christian music. We had our own home worship services where she chose the Scriptures. We practically lived in the church. We got involved in its ministries and its small groups, which became a faith family for us.

My daughter had so many questions about faith. Every week there was a new one, and we spent many hours in conversation about them. I tried not to duck any of them, though I was often stumped.

During her adolescence, she withdrew from the church, rebelling against all she had been taught. Though I prayed for her salvation daily, her faith was shattered in a Bible course taught by a priest who ridiculed her as "Miss Sunday School." But she never lost her love for Jesus—though she was sometimes afraid he had lost his for her.

When she became pregnant, she decided she wanted to follow him. She wanted to be a "good person" for her daughter and for herself. She came back to church and started to explore membership. She is learning to hear Jesus' voice for herself and to see his care in her life. She is a much happier person, too. I would be remiss if I did not thank God for this every single day.

Today I can see that the experience of being a single parent has taught me more about Jesus and given me more faith than anything else in my life. I was probably doing more learning than teaching. My daughter and I have shared the reality of God in our lives, as head of our home, as father and mother and lover and teacher and friend. That more than anything else is what we have lived on. Her faith and mine have grown together and supported each other like two trees. Without her need for love, her need to trust, my faith would be puny indeed.

"LORD, TEACH US TO PRAY"

That's what they asked him, if you can believe it.
Crafty Lover that he is, he did not reply—at least not right then,
"Okay, first there'll be a whole lot of pain and loss.
Then your children will begin to suffer.
Then your whole world will be shattered.
When those things happen, you will begin to pray."

No, he started off with the ABCs:
"Daddy, we love you! We trust you!"
"Daddy, forgive us—we forgive, too!"
"Daddy, save us, because you alone can!"
"Yes, yes, that's what we want!"

He started us children off easy,
Intimating it would be harder as we went along.
There would be crucifixions, his and ours.
There would be dying.

It was hard to believe that at first
From a person who was so full of joy,
Whose every request resulted in miracle.
But as we grew, we learned he spoke the truth.

He also said our sorrow would be turned to delight,
Our agony would bring great gain for the kingdom we prayed would come.
He spoke the truth in that, too, we learned.
And so we in our turn start the children out easy.
"Jesus loves me," we sing, and it is true.

We never quite see until we look back
How their hope and trust in us made us risk more, believe more
Than we ever could before.
Was it that way for him, too,
When they asked him to teach them?

Mi Hermana, Mi Hermana

*Hear this, you who trample the needy and do away with the poor of
the land, saying, "When will the New Moon be over that we may sell
grain, and the Sabbath be ended that we may market wheat?"—
skimping the measure, boosting the price and cheating with
dishonest scales, buying the poor with silver and the needy
for a pair of sandals, selling even the sweepings with
the wheat. The Lord has sworn by the Pride of Jacob:
"I will never forget anything they have done.
Will not the land tremble for this,
and all who live in it mourn?"*
Amos 7:4-8

I was raised in a biased environment. Unpleasant slurs on a person's
race, religion, ethnicity, or gender were commonplace. I did not want this
for my daughter; I'm glad we live in a neighborhood which is home for
people of many races.

My granddaughter's father is African-American, and I want her to
know and be proud of her heritage. But I need to learn more about it in
order to have anything to share with her.

A white friend of mine suggested subscribing to *Ebony* as a place to
start. There I find a whole world of art, literature, music, dance, history,
and learning to which I have never been introduced. What a pauper I am.
I only know things about white people living in Europe and North America.

My grandfather was a Cherokee. He died without my finding out
from him about my heritage. He suffered persecution because he was a
Native American but he never talked about it. My friend Lillie said, "You
wouldn't know how it was in the South when your children could only
play with white boys until age twelve and then were told they couldn't any
more and from then on they were to call the white boys 'mister.' "

She's right. Without her, I would never have known.

Our children must not grow up isolated from people of other races and cultures. They must not grow up hating or fearing difference. The racial violence we see is the product of generations of this kind of thinking and acting. Instead of making jokes about people who are not like us, and pushing them away from us, we need to help our children see how people who seem very different are like us in the most important ways. We and they need to value and appreciate the differences in people.

Charlotte, an Asian-American, suggests that we try not to think in terms of having everyone be the same, but of needing "one of every kind to make a complete set." Becky suggests classifying things by similarities rather than by differences.

We also need to relearn our history. United States wealth came from exploiting the riches of a land taken by force and deceit from Native Americans. Later much U.S. wealth was derived from the forced labor of people of color. Today much of our wealth (and food) comes from mistreatment of laborers who are illegal immigrants and from sweatshops all over the world. To have pride in what they inherit from us, all of our children need to know this and to see us working for justice and change.

MI HERMANA, MI HERMANA

My sister, I must tell you,
The beautiful flowers your lover sends you
Are killing me, killing the child within me.
I know you care, but you are so far away.

The doctor says (not the company one)
I am sick because of the toxins they spray
On your flowers so each will be perfect.
The perfect flower I keep under my heart
Is sick, too, the doctor says, and may not live
To see the light of her first day.

Oh, my sister, I must tell you of the bitter tears
Full of man-made poisons,
That fall to my pillow each night.
I must tell you, because you are so far away
That if I did not tell you, you would not know.
I know that if you knew, you would care.

Our cousins, our uncles and aunts, our padriños,
They, too, are sorrowing, I must tell you
Because of the food you must eat
And the clothes you must wear.
Cruel men have taken their land
To grow your coffee, chocolate,
Bananas and pineapples, steers,
Cotton and coconuts, rubber and twine.

Oh my sister, if only you could see,
I know it would break your heart.
Forgive these few words—the tears have started again.
I wanted to be in touch with you
From so far away
And to tell you I love you
Before I am too sick to write any more.
Please remember me in your prayers
As I remember you in mine.

Mortality

Fathers, do not exasperate your children; instead, bring them up in the training and instruction of the Lord.
Ephesians 6:4

Sister Adelia Milligan, a family therapist who worked with us, taught me an invaluable lesson. She explained that being able to do something, or "mastery," is an indispensable part of self-esteem.

If I do something for my daughter that she is able to do for herself, I rob her of a chance to add to her self-esteem. Sister Adelia states it as a rule: "Never do anything for anyone that she can do for herself." Resentment over this kind of theft often provokes our children to wrath.

Even a little reflection on my own childhood bears this out. I was always one to "do it by SELF!" So is my daughter. It took me a long time to learn how to cope with this as a parent, however.

On many a snowy morning, my daughter used to wake up late and ask to be driven to school. I would do so, often coming in to work late because of it, but I would inwardly fume. If I said no, I felt guilty when she cried, "Other mothers drive their kids to school!" I would change my mind. I took her but was angry about being manipulated.

One morning I decided she could walk to the city bus stop and make her own excuses to the school administration. The emotions were violent that morning! But after a few more such instances, I was amazed to discover that she could indeed wake up on time by herself. All I needed was to stop taking care of her. The biggest payoff was that she was pleased with herself, too.

When her daughter was born, they lived with us for six months. Our idea was to help her. But secretly she resented still living at home. She and my granddaughter now live in a studio apartment three blocks away, thanks both to our community and her own hard work and struggle.

She is so happy about this arrangement. She said to me, "I know you feel sad that I don't want to live with you. But when I do, I ask you for things and you do them. When I'm by myself, I have to do it on my own. It feels so good when I solve my own problems and do things I've never done before."

It is wonderful to see how this gets translated into my granddaughter's life. She is a little girl who obviously feels secure. Her mom doesn't hover over her, protecting her from every conceivable harm (although she doesn't neglect her either).

She is learning there are many things she can handle by herself. Yet when she recently tumbled off a step and her head got caught underneath a folding chair in the next row of seats in the church, she never made a sound. She just waited patiently for her mother to come and extricate her. She knows that when she really needs help, it will be there.

I can just see the smile on Jesus' face. This is how he wants her to be—confident in herself and trusting that she will be cared for. It's what he wants for all his kids, old and young.

MORTALITY

Oh, my God,
You are like the sea,
Echoing with mystery,
Calling, calling.

Resistless we are drawn
Into your net.
You advance, we retreat.
When you flee, we pursue,
As helpless against your weakness
As against your strength.

And like the sea,
When you speak in roar or whisper,
Your voice throbs in all our veins,
Nor can we help but recognize
In you our homely source.

But yet! oh, my God,
For all your calling
There is this—
We are mortal,
And you have never known an end.
When the riptides of the Spirit run,
We are drawn in to die,
And we have only your word after that.

Like the sea on a bright day,
You laugh at our caution.
And young in our strength
Or wise in our acceptance,
Arms wide, hearts open, our names surrendered,
One by one, we present ourselves
To the flood of your light.
Our names float like pearls on your tide.

1 Corinthians 13:4-8

But the greatest of these is love.

1 Corinthians 13:13

This morning I read a heartrending story in the newspaper. A judge took a woman's three sons from her and gave custody to the father because she had no job and way of providing for them. Their father moved to another state with the boys.

Her reaction was amazing. She has done her best to keep in touch with her sons. She writes to them, phones them each week, and calls their school and asks to be informed of their progress. She affirms their successes at school, stays in touch with their teachers, and has even arranged to be a "homeroom parent," sending treats for each son's class.

She has accepted enforced distance but not emotional separation. She is still their mother. She still does what she can to mother her sons. She encourages everyone in her situation to be the best long-distance parent he or she can be. The children's welfare is worth the sacrifice.

Here is another story. Someone I know has had several abortions. Her boyfriend is a drug addict. The last time she got pregnant, she decided to keep the baby. Her parents said she couldn't do that and live with them. They insisted on adopting the baby themselves and coerced her into giving up her rights as a parent.

They insist that she call the baby her sister. Her parents are sending her to college far enough away that she can come home only on weekends. In between she has painful phone conversations with her child, who cries for her to come home. This causes the parents to berate the daughter for upsetting the child. They tell her not to call any more and hang up.

In which case is the child's welfare primary?

All parents get angry at their children. All parents get tired and wish their own needs could be met. One exhausted single mom told me, "I wish somebody would feed *me*, give *me* a bath, put *me* to bed." Perhaps in no situation does this hit so hard as when parenting alone.

But these small, unformed individuals have no one but us to love them. They are loaned to us by God for a few very short years. We are responsible to love them. When we do or say things to them that are wrong, we must repent and ask their forgiveness. This is not weakness—it is the greatest kind of teaching we can do.

As my friend Anne says, "Children do not so much learn from what we say as from who we are." If we want them to be loving adults, we must make the necessary sacrifices to become loving parents. First Corinthians 13 is a guide or checklist to help us stay on the right track.

1 CORINTHIANS 13:4-8

Love is patient,
  love is kind.
It does not envy,
  it does not boast,
  it is not proud.
It is not rude,
  it is not self-seeking,
  it is not easily angered,
  it keeps no record of wrongs.
Love does not delight in evil
  but rejoices with the truth.
It always protects,
  always trusts,
  always hopes,
  always perseveres.
Love never fails.

The Author

Susanne Coalson Donoghue was a single parent for sixteen years. Leaving her family and her birthplace in California in 1977, she and her two-year-old daughter joined Reba Place Fellowship in Evanston, Illinois, a covenant Christian community which practices income sharing and common decision-making.

Although she has been writing poetry since 1962, Susanne's main preoccupation has been earning a living for herself and her daughter. She has held many jobs, from scrubbing floors to floral design to tax accounting. In January, 1990, she received a master's degree in pastoral studies from Loyola University of Chicago. In 1991, she self-published her first book of poetry, *A Perfect Season*.

Until recently she was administrative assistant for Evangelicals for Middle East Understanding at North Park College. She offers spiritual direction and edits a meditation guide for covenant communities in her spare time. She is still a member of Reba Place. She is recently married and has one grandchild. She is blessed extravagantly by the generous sisters and brothers who have chosen to be her friends. Her favorite thing is being alive.